D1085398

Jugglers and Tides

Jugglers and Tides

Poems by
Priscilla Orr

HANNACROIX CREEK BOOKS

Stamford, Connecticut

FIRST EDITION

Library of Congress Catalog Number: 96-79972

ISBN: 1-889262-02-1

Publisher's Cataloging in Publication
(Prepared by Quality Books Inc.)
Orr, Priscilla.
      Jugglers & tides / Priscilla Orr.
      p. cm.
      ISBN: 1-889262-02-1
      I. Title. II. Title: Jugglers and tides.
   PS3565.R777J84 1997   811'.54
                      QBI96-2565

HANNACROIX CREEK BOOKS

1127 High Ridge Road, #110
Stamford, CT 06905
(203)321-8674   FAX (203)968-0193
e-mail: Hannacroix@aol.com
on the web: http://www.bookzone.com/HannacroixCreek

Printed in United States of America

In memory of my mother
Patricia Sanderson Cottley

Contents

III

Floundering

The men crept down the shore,
their small circle of lights beaming
around their dark shapes like old Albertine
who'd wander through the dark school courtyard
her rusty prong spearing Gold Brick candy paper.
The men would shine their light
on some poor flat fish pulsing
in the low tide bed. The shape

of their floppy hats shifted toward
the bay bridge. Its green lights
formed a flickering arc over the coal
black Gulf. I'd sit at the edge of the pier
my saddle oxfords dangling
until the boards cut into my thighs.
Cars whirred back and forth
from New Orleans to Pass Christianne.

One of those could be my mother coming.
One of those could be her car.

Orchids

The cymbidium are the first I've bought
since our wedding. They sit in that glass
creamer that never poured right. Now
divorced longer than married, I can buy
this stem of them. They trailed
down my dress. I couldn't hold them
without my hands trembling.

You in your new suit, your lower lip puckered up,
chewing your mustache as you waited
under the hand-woven canopy. My errant dad
in his polyester western suit,
finally walking with me.

All day we waited for four o'clock.
Seconds before the ceremony, I could not
catch my breath. In that little bathroom
with the washer and drier, I had to stop,
take two gulps of air before coming to you
One of those blossoms got caught,
fell into the wicker wastebasket.

Time has given me a tenderness
for our failing. I picture you
with your sons and wonder why
I'm still out here.

I want another wedding,
a simple ceremony with friends and food.
I want to vow all those things I vowed
with you. As for flowers,
perhaps something less delicate,
like the tiger lily growing wild in my yard.

Low Tide on the Gulf, 1956

My bathing suit was cotton with two violet strands
to secure my top. You, afraid to bathe,
turned me over to your gentleman friend.
We walked the sand bars
until you were merely a speck on the shore.
Pleaséd by the wet silt squished through my toes,
I did not want him to pick me up. But as the water deepened,
he did. He untied my straps to see if I had breasts yet.
I squirmed, blubbered, looked over his shoulder for you.
I scared him. Why tell you now when you're dead?

It's this man I met at a wedding:
the one in the cream linen shirt
who danced with me in the rain,
who put his arm around me, twirled me, cradled me.
We found a table under the tent, a green glass candle
half-lit his face. He held my hand till I could speak.
Then he let it go.

I don't know which ones to keep.
Frozen in nine-year-old time,
my bare child's chest underneath these breasts
I keep letting them slip by.
If you could send me a gardenia, Mother,
if you could help me spill myself into this world.

Desire

Some nights nuns robed in black habits
return to chide me — do not chew the host.
Swallow it whole. It hurts Christ
if He touches my teeth. I gag him down
but he sticks to the roof of my mouth,
then melts away. At benediction
the altar boy holds up the silver
links of the incense burner,
clicking it against the gilded ball.

A gust of white smoke permeates
the altar mingling with Gregorian chant.
One white sock slides down his ankle,
but he can't reach back to adjust it.
On his knees, he loops his other loafer over
that sagging sock, trying to drag it up,
peering up at the priest who hates him to fidget.

When I wake to a blustery day, odor of cum
on the fingers of my right hand, the sun
flits in and out of the cumulus. From the window,
I spot rubbish scattered along the shoreline,
high tide marked by seaweed and remnant pieces of
    shell.
Only the smell of rotting fish and salt water come
    up.

Long after, the dreamed incense simmers
like a young girl's sin whispered
to the dark shape of a priest.
Bent toward the sliding screen
between them, he can feel her breath
nestling in his ear.

Skittish

(for Margo)

Every time she wants him,
she bites into anything carbohydrate.
Lately it's been spelt bread.
Sensing his impact on her, he delights
in how her nipples harden beneath
her sheer silk blouse when they casually speak.
Once he came up behind her desk,
stroked the back of her neck with his fingertips.

He does not see flabby pock-marked thighs,
only the meaty curve under her skirt
which he would clutch under him
given the chance. But the fat girl
appears ruthless in her mirror,
and she can't shake that image from her sleep.

She remembers a dress: red-bridled white ponies
all rearing up in a kind of dance. Mother
stands her on a chair to be pinned, tucked, and
    snipped,
yellow tape measure curled to the floor.
When it's finished, she twirls around,
    giggling, light-headed.
Such a pretty little girl, a neighbor says,
her mother's murmur of agreement barely audible.

Voyeur

At twenty-five she was hot,
emerald green body suit, 'O-positive' nail polish,
and always the wine. A man wandered
into her lavender mirrored bedroom
and as she arched her back over him,
he would tease her nipples with his tongue.

When she began to seduce death,
I stepped back, offered to toss the gallon Chablis
        jugs
that lined her garage walls. During a sober period,
she found a half-filled wine goblet rancid
among cleansers under her bathroom sink.

My body vomits grape, grain or sperm, any nectar
I crave. It cannot plummet head down into the abyss
in one wild gesture toward death. It cannot
        discriminate
between a man who'd drip hot wax over my
        buttocks
from the thick thumbed one
who'd knead the bottoms of my feet.

She called once from the hurricane center,
said her roof collapsed, said she'd sat the night
in drenched carpeted chaos trying to decide to live.
She called a year later, her voice inaudible.
I told her not to call again.

First String

Because I was tall, they made me pivot guard.
My bumbling body couldn't articulate
the language of dribbling. I wanted to be
Jo Mary Artigues, first string. Her squat body
propelled itself around my knees,
leapt up to the goal. She'd make the sign
of the cross before a foul shot. God glided
her balls through the net while mine
deflected off the rim. At eleven,

I needed a miracle. But each time
I got the ball some little disaster
would occur, it would get smacked out
of my hands, the thief dribbling away.

I think about Jo Mary,
wonder how her life worked out,
what she did when basketball
was no longer respectable for a young girl.
I still hesitate to take a foul shot.
But I've gone back to fall in love with that
      gangly girl,
the one who tried too hard.
I coach her in the long languorous way of her body.

Lighthouse at Barnegat Bay

The ranger unlocks the door
and we climb the spiral staircase
to the top. A rubber band holds
his hair in one clump, splitting
into it. Does he argue with his wife?
Does she try to get him to wear
those colored elastic circles
that protect the hair?

A tide table's taped to a wall.
The tide moves out,
turbulence impossible to see.
He talks about Camille,
how one survivor who held on all night
to a tree, skin ripped from her arms
and legs, her body in shock,
was acquitted years later
—hurricane trauma—
for ax murdering her husband.

This ranger's like a man I loved once,
so limber so light his brogans
weigh him down. He pours coffee
careful to give me the cup
with fewer chips in the lip.
What about that woman, I ask,
the one who married and loved.
No wind today, he says.

Who knows when the wind will come up,
or a riptide will fling a body smack into a jetty,
batter it against the rocks before dragging it up
on the shore? She went out into the storm
meaning to find refuge before it took hold.

Living Alone

Forced to ascend,
through bear grass, lupine, bitterroot,
I find the rich cup of Indian Paintbrush
splayed over the glacial meadow.

The thaw begun — streams swell
and sputter down the mountain,
a grizzly lumbers over the high meadow.
I cradle my hand around the delicate red folds
pick it, twirl it round my cheek.

Hiking near the glacier, wet snow
under the summer sun, how do I know
if like my mother
I slip too deeply into myself...
Bound over glistening white ice,
how do I know
that I haven't looked into that liquid
we call love and named you in it.

Promise to a Friend with Cancer

Knowing nothing about plants
I water your amaryllis angelique.
In the white blossom a trace of pink
widens into a slight vein.
Plant the bulb in spring, you tell me,
but what do I know of the earth.
Inept, I cheat her, plan cremation;
let no worms make their way
through a satin–lined coffin.

This death talk hid itself
during our St. Regis high tea:
clotted cream, freshly–baked scones,
a little gossip, a negotiation over dessert.
While you nibbled through the patter of voices,
a familiar hunger took hold—
to love, to be loved, to love.

Now, you fret over the plant,
make me snip its little pink tongues
that smudge my fingertips
with such sweet yellow grain.

If you'll let me smear your cheek with it—
streaked orange mask,
uneven seam dried into us,
binding , splicing, tracing its own way,
I will plant that blasted bulb of yours.

Cisco

I found her by a diner in New Paltz,
 a scrap of a thing. Fed her cat food in the morning,
shared my supper with her at night.
Always, she ate.

Now, her scent fails her.
She can't find a chicken morsel dropped on the floor.
In the wild, some dog would tear her throat apart.

I heard how a man held his cat
while the vet injected it,
held her till the fluid flooded the life out of her.

I try to ready myself for it,
her little body going slack in my arms.
It keeps me kind to her.

Cabin Porch at Dusk

That loon is wailing for its lost mate.
I'm wrapped in your ragged red blanket,
the one thing I could not discard, your odor,

replaced by burnt pine cones from my fire.
Somewhere in the city, you sit with your mate.
I like to think you do not lean into one another

when the temperature drops, or that your short
    grey beard
doesn't chafe against her breasts. This is not love,
this ever present desire I have for you.

But when that loon wail pierces the quiet,
I cannot distinguish it from my own loss.
If you name your marriage love:

that habit of waking to a rhythm,
coffee, crossword, children-to-school, why
does your checkered-green screen

lit with messages from all over the world,
summon me? What wildness tapped
in solitary blips of your keyboard
only emerges at night, your wife asleep upstairs?

With no creature cry
for my own fierce uncoupled love,
I take hunks of bread

scatter them across the twilight
hoping that loon will get them,
hoping it will find sanctuary among its own kind.

Aravaipa Canyon Elegy

Your dog runs the canyon
collecting cactus burrs
in her nose. I fumble
trying to get them out.
She yelps, pulls away.
You would hold her long mouth
in the palm of your hand,
remove each burr
with barely a wince from her.
I try. But my hand

cannot steady this creature.
We ride the jeep together
looking for some sign of your spirit.
An eagle circles over us;
the still motion of its glide
settles the canyon silence within me.

There's something in my dreaming,
how I wake each morning hungry for sex.
Last night, I sat naked
in front of a mirror,
curly mass of hair
above the open lips
of the dulcet dark slit.

I saw what men must see
your death bringing me
to love this meager body,
my belly, my breasts
drooped into a womb-like curve.

Ashes in a little gold–papered box
dowsed with holy water,
you are a baptism of desire.
In the haze of grief,
I see you at the sink,
crutch tucked under your arm
washing straw from a single brown egg,
and I bless me. Each month,
I see clots of blood
in the faded porcelain bowl,
I bless me. Each day
I wake in the heat
of a dream, I baptize me.
In the name of no father,
no son...

Dusk

Snow fell in the desert this year,
White coating on spiny cactus limbs.
All day long, kids ran in-and-out,
shouting snow, snow.
I watched from the window,
the imprint of their feet
scattered everywhere.

By nightfall, the ground
had swallowed every drop.
But just after the sun
set behind the mountains,
words like Running Deer or Quicksilver
settled in the chilled air.

With no image for your grave,
I drew your name into me the way
I pull in the humming behind
a friend or lover's word.
Still damp from the snow,
the ground bore the pattern
of tiny footprints. As sure

as the sun would dry it,
wipe out every trace
of those steps, I knew

the ground would yield.
At dusk, an underground feeder

would surface through the hot crust of earth
form an invisible mist
that would whisper your name.

An Obsession With Murder

My mother read thrillers, her favorite
a well-spoken detective always a bit drunk,
a bit in trouble with his superior.
Abandoned by his wife, he wandered
from one body to the next. Usually a woman,
the corpse would be found, her body sprawled
over a mattress, on a tiled floor. Our hero,
always too late on the scene, would cover her,
then hunt down her killer. I see my mother,
her bed light too low, always reading,
entering the world of that man, as if turning
each page was a way of gathering him to her.

Death she would have called to her
if this kind unsteady man came with it.
In our longing, the fumbler's always enough.
His hairline recedes, his head bows.
Sweet insistent desire never too close.
And the imperfect men who love us
stare into the dusk-lit yard wondering.

II

Debris

It starts with you
and mother fumbling
together, her, a naive twenty

just from Cambridge
stiff and scared
hating sex. You, immense,

from South Philly.
Your clumsy hands
hold onto her,

trying to be gentle.
But she lays waiting
for it to be over.

You thrust harder
until you are beyond her.
I come from the collapse

of your bodies. Not love,
but some angry seed
spilled into her.

Unborn Daughter

Your egg lives within me
growing weary of the wait.
I thought you'd be here
by now. But daughter, I choose wrong.
There's been no man wanting the fall
of your red hair. I scare men.

The nuns were no help.
Black–robed figures, gliding
over oak floors, their beads
clicked down the hallway.
We slept in rows, each nun cloistered
by a white curtain, the shadow
of their undressing flung onto the wall.
I'd wait for their light to go out
before I'd sleep, then grab Bear.
Together we'd ride magnolia–scented
nights. If we moved too hard
the nuns would holler, make me stand
at the foot of my bed, arms folded
till I promised to squirm no longer.

But magnolia air is thick.
I'd crawl into the chapel,
sit under the Virgin, her candles burning,
beg her to bury my need.
Her long blue robe fell over me,
quelling the magnolia.
I became the sweet white flower with no scent.

Mysterious men,
I am clumsy before them.
But to know your egg could wither
before your hair burns red
tightens my every muscle.

Obsession

And what if an old woman sits at the window
waiting for her granddaughter to come
bouquet of wild flowers spilling over her arms
or the thin redhead home from the office
with the face of a man called Evan pressed into her
      sleep.
What if no-one cares for them
or cares for the benched boy in Little League
who practices his time *at bat* every waking moment.

My spaniel, nose down, haunches taut,
hunkers down after some scent.
Danger dreamer, I tell myself,
how the world spins its curved mirror around me.

What if your tongue could open my labia,
tease the engorged pink tissue to release itself,
what harm could come from such a tenderness.
I heard if you pray to St. Philomena ten days
      straight,
she'd answer the impossible, then heard she's
      uncanonized.
Who can pray with such certainty?
Who can trust the gods to show themselves to us?

The Blue Mug

His niche faces a courtyard,
open sky, desert, then mountains.
He chose it, you tell me.
Said he could die easier
knowing he'd come to a place like this.
I see the two of you
sitting on a cement bench,
hands clutched together,
your eyes filling up.
You'd have swallowed hard,
as you walked back to the car.

At home, after the cemetery,
I spy his little blue mug nestled on the shelf.
The first lesson in grief and I almost fail,
wanting to move it for you.
Each routine habit now sears into your day:
taking down two mugs,
waiting for the kettle to whistle.
Stirring one mug, then the other,
you'd make your way to the bedroom,
the hot liquid lapping up and down
Molly following, her tail
wagging in time to your step.

Three days, it takes. I wake to find
a clean spoon resting on a folded paper towel.
You've kept the water just beneath boiling.
When I reach for my mug,
the little blue one is gone,
moved into a shadow on the top shelf.

Living Alone II

My married friends tell me
it's the same for them, the silence,
how the soul keeps trying to find itself.
But I still look for you.

Last night I thought I saw you
in a bookstore. You had Rilke
in your hand. Your long lean body
seemed to rock itself as you stood there.
All these years without sex,
I might have followed you home,
fumbled with your shirt as we climbed the stairs.

All I needed was some sign.
You could have read me a line or two.
You could have placed your hand on my cheek.

Dancer

On Sunday night Maud's Starfire Lounge
closes down for men in unbuttoned collars
and dress whites. The girl wants to wear red.
But Maud finds it tawdry for private parties,
pulls an emerald chemise from the chifferobe.

Sitting on a stool in front of a globe-lit mirror,
while her mother draws the brush down her back,
she imagines herself in a music video.
Her clothes like quavering petals
fall from her arched silhouette. Yanking out
the tangled clumps of dark hair, Maud

readies her, then lifts the dress over her. Plump
little breasts remain free to sway up from the cloth.
Each dip and whirl reveal enough thigh
to make the young ones gasp, to pull all eyes
through the cigarette haze to her. Even the women
long acquainted with Maud's are compelled by the
    tease.
Already it comes too easily to her, but for the
    money.

Later, if she's lucky, a drunk one will succumb
on the dressing room cot in a blathered burst.
It's the fierce who rip and sting their way into her,
while shy ones linger until the waves come.
Once when she could not lose herself, she heard
the jangling of her mother's step just outside the
    door.

Amazing Grace, how sweet the sound
that saved a wretch like me...
John Newton, 1725-1807
played by Hubert Laws on Morning Star

Cafe Tres Bien

It was raining hard that Friday night
mid-April. We were caught
cotton soaked and cold, five dollars between us.
The coffee shop with the French name,
like the neighborhood, was in transition:
a copper espresso maker among dark pine tables
names of lovers scratched or scribbled into the
    wood.

Chilled, you wrapped your arms around yourself,
wet blonde hair matted down your cheeks.
"No rush, no rush," said the Jamaican waiter
so we drank our coffee staring at the rain-driven
    street.
My lover had left; yours was married.
We sat in the long time silence of old friends
adding a fragment to a thought expressed hours ago.

How far we were from Montana, always lost,
always driving miles looking for a bar to serve us.
Here we were again at Cafe Tres Bien,
the waiter stacking chairs onto tables.

45

But when that flute came over the radio,
we held still in our shivering; even the waiter
    stopped.
Bittersweet, filling the room with a sadness older
than us all, what strange comfort it gave.
As we huddled together
our cups filled one last time,
I watched the waiter, so at ease
as he wiped down the counter,
so at ease in this room with us.

The Reservoir

A pregnant woman walks her Golden Retriever,
an older dog. Familiar companions, they make
   their way
through the rusted peeled-back fence.

Soon she will not fit.
The dog will leap through,
wag its tail from the other side
and she will struggle with her bulk
not wanting to disappoint him,
but she will have to stop.

Her husband, much less patient,
will shorten the dog's walk time,
yank its lead when they get to the opening in the
    fence.
He's like that man in the tan uniform
who comes in the Newark Water Truck
to thread closed the hole with red-covered wire.

I once visited a woman in the nursing home nearby.
On her night table sat a 50's photo of her: in pasties,
short satin shorts and strapped heeled shoes,
a hat with plumage spraying over her head.
"It's not a dirty picture," she said to me
before slipping into incoherence.

Portrait of my Mother

She struggles to sit up.
Skin around the incision puffs up,
a crude red ridge down her chest.
Her feet dangle over the edge of the bed,
another gash trailing down her thigh
where they took the vein. It drains a little on the
    bedsheet.
Her left hand grips the tray table as she steadies
    herself.

She gazes beyond me.
Little tremors heave through her body,
and I get a bedpan. When I change her gown,
I see for the first time the flat skin
where there is no breast.
Startled by the smoothness,
by the way the body compensates
for its own loss, I turn away.

In Montana, in the rolling plains,
snow glimmering under the moon,
a voice could shriek out into the silence
over the rolling hills, but hear
its own sound muffled in the expanse.

Shame

The day we expelled Tommy Tate, he had come
into the Math Center to work on fractions.
Like my father, lumbering and tall,
he walked with head bowed. At the hearing,
he uttered inaudibly, how he'd once found a wallet
full of cash and credit cards and turned it all in.
"I'm not a bad person," he kept saying.
Nick, his more savvy partner from Newark,
was ready to deal. We did it. We're Black
from the Projects, this our only chance.

At eight years old, I wet the bed.
Sister Leonard huffed and grumbled,
made me strip the mattress, place my palm
on the wet spot not yet yellowed.
You should have a rubber sheet, she told me
in the flurry of changing linen.
A baby sheet. Wisps of black hair slipped
out from her veil, her squat body flapping
a clean sheet in the air. I stood at the foot
of my bed, arms folded, shamed by the stink
in my pajamas. I prayed not to do it again.
But my urine quietly spilled three more times,
unlike the clattered crowing of the Gethsemeni cock.

Tommy knows that private garden,
where Judas invariably makes his way.

Heritage

When he played Bach, invariably he'd stumble,
then came the long string of unintelligible curses.
I'd be at the sink doing dishes hungry for him to
    go on.
How he'd ended up at some Minuteman Missile site
guarding silos at 40 below,
never troubled me.

He ate my burnt hot dogs or took me out
for cube steak sandwiches. That he was my ally
when I wanted to wear stretch pants, or stay out
    later,
that he sang Broadway show tunes through the
    house,
made me certain I would be safe.

They aren't all like the man on the beach
who leer when your mother looks away.
Sometimes, you have little love names for them
like Pudgy Bear or they do a silly dance
to mimic a go-go girl in her white boots.
They don't aim to stake claim to your body,

nor do they think about the men who come later,
the ones who reach out for you in the dead of night
only to feel your long legs tighten involuntarily
as the moon absents itself from your window.

A Walk in the Columbia County Woods, Winter '93

To hear the creek sputtering under the ice floe,
to see the grove so spare in the snow,
dropped boughs frozen before the spring decay,
you'd think the Eastern hemlocks would live
forever. Even a fallen sprig seems alive
its fragile needles don't prickle
as I smooth it out in my palm.

So much failure in the world: Jackie,
a mother at 15, begs me to keep her from beating
her baby. Renee goes back to her man,
only to be found 40 stab wounds later,
stuffed in a plastic bag under her bed.
Rodney with the light black skin
blows off his only job.

Under barely murmuring boughs,
my dog runs ahead seeking out a scent,
in the fresh yielding snow.
She does not try to save anything.

Chasing Spirits: A Journey on the Lost Inca Trail

1.

Your clear notes fall over the Andes
like some Inca priest calling his people home.
Air is scarce at this altitude. Ruins un-restored.
Weeds grow through cracked rock while the ghost
of an Inca warrior, with his dream of foiling
the Spaniard, bids me to lay down my pack.
But your music pulls me toward you,
past the llama wandering these trails.

2.

My sleeping bag cast under a ruin
provides shelter against the night air.
Orange peel and an empty brandy bottle
tell me I don't journey alone. Your music
a lonely string in a chamber of mountains
tugs at the pit of my stomach.
I can't get warm.
I want you here not your music,
and I dream I won't find you
at the end of your flute. My legs ache.
Hunger works through my sleep
as I lean closer to the rock for comfort.

3.

Urubamba river sidles below,
a flash of mercury in the brief sunlight,
one moment visible, one moment not.
A German woman, Gabi, in a Cusco cafe
gave me espresso, thick bread with strawberry jam,
warned me: the lack of oxygen once made a woman
leap from the mountain, pressure in her head
so great. Chew cocoa leaves, my friend said.
Don't do this alone. Light-headed I walk.
For miles, no sign of you.
But on my last night, in a straw-covered hut
the stone city just below me,
the sound of a quena weaves through my sleep.
I dream I am in Newark airport,
rummaging through my knapsack
colored tissue everywhere,
and your gift left somewhere in Peru.

Prayer Basket

When Mary Ann put our names in the prayer basket,
I knew we had a chance
our little white slips of paper mingling with the
    others —
a man with cancer, the woman who'd had an affair.
I imagined each hand passing the wicker basket,
dropping in an appeal. I'm amazed

at what I can't see like the Yield sign
I've driven by for six years, and me
yelling at all those drivers, swerving
into their lane. Why is the sign only now clear?
What has shifted my life into slow motion?

Not knowing what you'll do, I putter,
remove dried leaves from the spider plant
or grind my Tanzania Peaberry beans.
Mostly, I talk to my cat, tell her how
any minute that slip of paper could get pulled
right out of the basket,
a kind of lottery for dreams.

Blue Curtains

(for my mother)

It was the way the afternoon light
would filter into the bedroom
that made her want blue curtains.
To him, it made no sense.
Make them all the same color.
But each time she'd lie down
on the day bed with her book
she'd rest her eyes a moment,
imagine a blue cast of light flowing
over her. When he died
I offered to buy them for her.
But she couldn't allow it.
The day she was born, her mother
left the hospital never to return for her.
The day she died, they'd moved her
to a room with rattan curtains
opening onto the mountains beyond.
They'd built a box over her legs
to keep the blankets from crushing
what little circulation she had left.
A deep wine-colored cushion
between her and the mattress
protected her skin. I wiped
her brow with a cool white washcloth.

In the cafeteria I ate a chili dog
and when night came I clutched my relic
of a rosary in one hand, held her hand
in the other not knowing what to say.
The television went on inanely.
But what has all this to do
with a pair of blue curtains
or the way her body, finally emptied of her,
seemed so familiar to me.

Divorce

Always the stronger swimmer
when I felt you falter,
I reached my arm
over your chest,
began the long swim
home. Your body trembled,
its weight wearing me down.
I summoned all my strength
to bring us in.

It was later, shore in sight,
that my arm ached.
For just one moment
I longed to backstroke,
to let the water carry me,
sun moving over for moon,
my legs opening
to the pull of a stronger tide.

If I let go,
it's that my arm wouldn't hold,
the white foam
lapping over my feet
seemed like home.

Veteran's Cemetery

(for my father, Clarence Robert Orr)

I hate that you're buried here,
miniature flags spattered over the mountainside.
My name on your marker stuns me,
a little plastic thing stuck in gravel,
and I have nothing to say to you.

You're like that man in the diner this morning
belly bulging over his belt. He took a stool,
ordered ham-n-eggs, sunnyside up,
chain smoked between gulps of coffee.
The waitress called him "sweetie"
and he smiled that weary smile of yours.

Here's where I fumble
where I want to lie,
to blame your failed life
on some failed flag.

You're the man
who sneezed behind the refrigerator
while mother and I giggled,
and then you were gone.

Wanting Normal

Desire's everywhere: the burnt sienna polish
of an older woman's toes, the boy stepping
up to bat — his father in the bleacher behind
home plate, the girl who places her phone
under a pillow.
Always possibility...

I keep wanting your long skinny fingers to
fumble with my vest, or to come home to me
full of daily complaint, your hand sliding
down me — an unconscious gesture of
married life.

Forty-six years it took to be heard. In a room
filled with secrets, we speak: one raped by
her brothers, one with dark ringlets who
cannot refuse any man, one who was
blackmailed to have sex while another
watched. These are the ones long schooled
in the body, the ones who came to know
themselves through a man's need. Now, the
unlearning of their sex is a passage back
through the tunnel of their girlhood. Others
like me are frozen. One woman protects
herself with bread and cake, her wedding
band wedged into the thick flesh of her
finger. Another stopped making love only
days after she married.

Some women my age curl into their hus-
bands, desire, a familiar dance exuding the
warm smelly sweat of an afternoon nap.

When they leave the bed loosely made, each
wanders into solitary pleasure — a book, a
snack, a phone call.

What was the sweetness outside my little-
girl window, honeysuckle or magnolia?
Memory fails me. Weeds take over my
impatiens, overwhelm the garden, and all I
can do is curl into the August heat, a kind of
hibernation. Yet, who would have me grieve
my life away? If I'm not vigilant, the weeds
soak up all nutrients from the soil.

The Christmas Photo

You posed for me as you always had,
the strained smile all you could muster.
I snapped it quickly thinking it was the cold
that bothered you. This photo would be sacred—
our Christmas together. And snow in Tucson,
white flakes on cactus. I couldn't see through
the frame, feel the rhythm of your naked breath.

Later, you said you hid at the party
ashamed to bring your shell of a body
to the celebration of others.
To me, you looked great.

Months later, the film finally developed —
your photo comes back crisp and clear,
skeletal, skin drawn into your body,
arms lost in the lumbering sleeves of your
    blue-checked jacket.

The Living Room Set

I was fifteen when you got the living-room set,
already too tall for the little brown sofa.
The wooden legs wobbled whenever I sat too hard.
I was always sitting hard, my body spilling over
any chair or couch trying to settle itself.

What I saw was what I dusted,
the blue glass globe of a lamp,
the imprint of your purse
on the nubby fabric
after you' d leave for work.

This last visit home
I stretched out,
slung my legs over the new couch.
When you came into the room,
I jumped as if I were nine.
"Honey, it's okay," you said,
brought coffee to my side.

But later, after I went to bed,
in the dim night light,
you fluffed each cushion
so very carefully
as if this set would have to last.

Older Woman

His nineteen year old body
old jeans, cut off sweat shirt
sits across from me.
He rubs his hand across his thigh
at the weakness of my refusal.
If he reached over my desk
I might grab onto him,
let him take me down his block
to fall on a mattress
in his unfinished room.

No sex, I tell myself,
his lean brown body
limber, always moving just outside
my reach. I become what I crave:
a controlled spiral of desire
circling tightly into oblivion.

An Odd Elegy for my Mom

After an all night rain the sand clings to everything.
Shrimp boats are anchored for winter, their paint
	peeling.
Even my coffee's bitter. Why come back
to this ratty brown shore you loved. Why talk to you
as if you weren't dead. Last night, I hunted down
my old academy. No white stone building
— just a lot full of old oak and pecan trees.
No ghost of Sister Leonard, whistle click against her
	beads.
No ghost of a girl in a blue pleated skirt, scuffed
	oxfords.

My ex-husband has MS, a virus that gnaws away
the myelin coating of the nerve. Scar tissue hardens
over raw wound, all damage hidden until the ravage
	ends.
He can never know if he'll see again, or know
where the virus might erupt next,
his own immune system poised to destroy him.

If I throw this cup away, it will decompose
only into tiny beads of Styrofoam
that slip into the gullet of a catfish or crab.
My friend drinks two gallons of wine without
	stopping,
and I succumb in my own way, drink a toast to you.

Here's to you, my mom, if you can hear me.
Here's to this salt water Gulf that gets us all.

Grief

In winter, the Chinook winds lifted snow
from the bushes and deposited it
outside our basement apartment window.

These drifts blocked the evening sun
but for one fragment of light spilled
into the living room. I could hear

the cab door slam, your boots crunch
up the walk. After the snowfall —
ruts, dog urine, boot prints all froze.

Before attempting suicide, my friend
told me a memory: she is a child folded
into a living room curtain. She peers

through the venetian blind into the dark
waiting for the orphan wagon — the man
in crepe soled shoes who steps towards her.

They have shut your eyes, wiped the vomit
from your lips. While I sit next to your bed
a few drops of blood on the sheet turn brown

as they dry. You have quieted yourself,
my slack-faced angel; the mild night wind
fills the room as your cheek begins to cool.

Silences:
A Personal Narrative

After my mother died, I was closing up her house, going through her things, deciding what to take with me, what to discard. What I found was as surprising as what I didn't find: my baby shoes, some photos, a few cards, a poem I'd written for my stepfather, but not anything else from my childhood or adult life. With the exception of some photo albums boxed in the garage there was nothing from her entire life. But in the midst of some papers, I did find a small slip of creme colored paper, and on it in her own hand was written a biblical sounding quote which essentially said, "The good woman is always silent." To realize my mother who held on to so little would copy this down and then save this slip of paper was disturbing in the midst of my grief. For it brought home to me how silent she was, and how I then had shaped myself in opposition to that silence.

In 1924, she was born in St. Johnsbury, Vermont. Her mother, disenchanted with married life, walked out of the hospital without her, leaving her and her husband. My grandfather had to carry her home in a basket. He worked for the railroad. So he left my infant mother with the woman who ran the boarding house. My mother never told me this story. I had to find out from her stepmother who heard it from my grandfather, perhaps not the most reliable narrator.

Yet the story seemed to explain a lot about my mother's reticence toward life.

How do we come to love someone so absent? My sense of love was formed in it—an immense longing that still resonates within me. It's everywhere in my creative work—inchoate, visceral, a kind of guttural code that I can only seem to translate into a poem. In this way, my mom is always with me. When she died, a good friend told me to bring home the things she used daily, a dish towel, a pot holder. Occasionally, I still find a treasure in her cookbook with odd clippings from the Tucson newspaper. It's how I've come to know her mind. The silence in her like the silence in women of her generation was a silence that withheld—it withheld pain, and it withheld desire.

But silence can obviously be healing. Alone on the beach in winter, the rhythmic sound of the waves restores me. I hope my mother had some comfort in her solitude. To what degree, I will never know. What we were able to share were the simplest acts of daily life: food, dogs, a good mystery book. These objects connected us, gave us the substance of our conversation. A few of her books are on my shelf. Her dish towels and scorched pot holders are among my own, and that damn slip of paper I've mislaid. But it's here too, somewhere among my own things.

III

Making Love on Shelter Island

Just like this body of mine to find itself now
in the slight sag of my breasts,
to crave your sex as if it were sixteen.

Move your leg between mine.
Slip inside despite the cross currents,
despite how long I've condemned closed
my ragged cache. To kiss the scarred shoulder
where your stitches healed wrong
to bury my face in your graying chest hair
to fold my mouth around you
is to secure that last trace of afternoon sun.

Maybe it's an unwelcome angel
that breeds our feral tenderness.
Feel her cast herself across the room
so subtle you'd simply think it an afternoon gust
blustered in off the dock.
Clammy mantle settling over us,
she mimes the brine smell of the ocean
the faint lime talc matted under your arm.

Dog Mother

Who knows why I never had a child.
But I think about it,
like the day I came home to find
the heel strap on my black leather pump
chewed through. My spaniel pup oblivious
to her crime yelped with excitement.
I was finally home.
Thinking what the shoes cost,
I tossed the good one in the back of the closet
as if half a pair could be replaced.

She licked my ankles,
paced toward the door —
what was taking me so long
to get us out on our walk?
I scooped out doggy biscuits
from a jar on top of the fridge.

Later, when she shot down the beach after the gulls
and they sprayed up around her before scattering,
when I picked up the driftwood
with which we'd play fetch,
I wondered what had buried itself within me,
what had made me so terribly afraid.

Shoreline in the Late Afternoon

The shoreline erodes each year,
our one strip of sand
holding itself against the waves.

I plop down in my chair,
but you, the planner, stand
over yours, carefully digging-in

before sitting. How subtle this sunset
in the East. It's all in how the light
gives way to the teal shadow of a wave,

how its absence sharpens
the white crest against our old sea.
You hold up your fingers, survey

the damage, sand dulling the sheen
of the new rose polish. I pull
out my pad. Under your visor

you sit alert, awaiting the end
of my scribblings, as if my pen
were creating our peculiar silence.

Maybe we are this strip of sand, shifting,
wearing away in places, pulled by
some powerful tide. Or maybe I feel

that sun racing west to splay her orange
rays across the sky, leaving us in the deep
cool of our worn coast. When the light

angles itself this way, I know
this is as close as we get to it,
that transient tenderness we long

to make forever. Burrowed under
your beach towel, your breath steadily
marks time with mine.

Ocean Grove

Closed on Sunday mornings,
this beach belongs to the Methodists.
A man in a blue jacket will chase you off
if you trudge your beach chair down before noon.
They're losing hold,
but you'd never know from the little tents.
At night they glow like lit pumpkins
with geraniums and plastic saints standing guard
while women in pastel sweaters
and men in seersucker pants
stroll down to the Great Auditorium
for a gospel tune or two.

Nearby the ocean at high tide
deposits a yellow bile in its froth
before sliding back into itself.

Jugglers and Tides

To admit I love you,
I had to read about tides:
earth caught in a gravitational
tug-of-war between the sun and moon.
All whirl inescapably together.
Unlike the juggler who depends on precision,

theirs is a lopsided movement;
moon pulling on one side,
sun yanking at the other
while all oceans swell and fall.
Wouldn't it be clever

to make this metaphor work for us,
to claim this pull toward you some natural force.
You would choose the juggler
watch as he executes balance,
adding a fourth neon tumbler.

But I prefer a bedlam of elements,
the steady lapping of water against sand,
or a light nor'easter — waves billowing up —
reminding us how quickly our shoreline erodes.

If only you would coax me into my bed,
creme-colored sheets softened by too much
    laundering,
we might stave-off the inevitable.
Or the tidal current, always a variable,
could erupt, complicate navigation
just long enough to shift our course.

An Afternoon Wedding Party at the Shore

How cool that September Saturday,
when young women in teal dresses and two inch
    heels
waddled over the sand after bride and photographer.
Men in tuxes hovered around an ice chest
popped open Heineken cans. Waiting for the shoot,
a renegade bridesmaid chugged one on her
    collapsible stool.
The bride's unwrinkled face seemed caught
between the west-bound sun splayed over her,
and a rowdy wind swishing the veil round her throat.

Maybe his receding hairline made her groom
    seem older,
his tenderness palpable as he reached for her.
When the photographer called family
      down from the boardwalk
Mother in deep green and diamonds commandeered
the party except for Father, like a puffin in his tux.

But the groom had only his mother under his arm,
diminutive in pale peach, and he seemed to lift her
    off the sand.

Further down the beach, a weekend fisherman
standing in rough surf pulled in a three-foot bass.
He held the sequin scales up against the light
    for all to see.
Delighted his wife applauded — her smacking sound
like slapped surf against shore;
jeweled fish teetering between them.

At the Art Museum

Fleshy white body, plump breasts, nipples erect,
her hand thrust in the air to meet his — they're
   in a boat.
If his face had been angry, I'd have hated him.
But he smiled, his upturned mouth slightly shy,
as if he knew millions of us would come
to stare at his metal breast plate hovering above
her billowy bosom. Garish, my friend called it,
bold splashes of color swirling over them.

Bad taste I have, an instinct for the crude.
Once I sat for an art class hoping my body
would burgeon and bloom under conte crayon.
I've always wanted to be a painting,
to see my thighs on a museum wall
curved 'round a bowl of plastic fruit,
or pick up little postcards of my breasts
slipping out of a wine velvet robe
as if someone could take my sprawling body,
shape it, and return it to me in full bouquet.

Solitaire

(for Sandy)

1.

That day your mother lay dying
we were on the beach,
knowing and not knowing.
You think of crazy things in those times:
me — how the boardwalk tilted downward
like popsicle sticks kids glue together
to make a fort or a bridge.
You — Maya Angelou's red boots,
and how she takes them with her on stage,
all the women who went before her.

With my own mother not gone a year,
I struggled to tell you
how the dead inhabit us,
move into our marrow.
Like this February wind,
we were bone chilled
the moment we left their womb.
Now, down again to that raw cold,
we find an invisible cord cut
before we've unriddled
how their breath can simply stop.

2.

Occasionally, I drink cognac
right from the bottle
only allowing myself
a small amount. Remy Martin
fine VS champagne. I sip now,
take comfort in this near empty bottle
knowing I don't have the courage
to buy a large one, don't know where
the damage ends. I will buy VSOP
one day before I put the bottle away.
The night my mother died,
I bought Wild Turkey,
held up my arm in a grand toast —
then crawled under the covers of her bed,
her scent barely present. I cried
as I tried to sniff it in. Like a lover's
remnant of aftershave, the more I sought it,
the more it eluded me. My whole body
convulsed into a scream
that never left my mouth.
When I woke a few hours later,
the drink on the night table
watered-down by ice, I dumped it,
thought of the startled check-out kid
when I'd paid for the bourbon. My mom
just died, I told him, and whatever
anyone tells you, it's a bitch.

3.

Walking the dog near a makeshift rink,
ice spattered on the walkways, I stopped
to watch kids play ice hockey on the pond.
The silver glint of one's boy's blade
caught fire in the afternoon sun
then dulled again as the cloud
eclipsed the slim shiny propeller.

Salt ate into the pads of Buddy's feet.
She favored one until she stepped in snow,
soothed them in the ice patches.
Then she'd rummage for a sodden branch,
her black nose covered in crystals.
Even though it was too cold,
I sat on the bench while she chewed,
thought back to the boy scraping
the pond with his stick, his small round puck
skidding by the others. Good shot.
This kid could close in on the goal,
bolt into a shadow while the black circle
traveled into an imagined net. I don't know

why this pleased me, nor why I sat
in the freezing sun, while bundled-up women
racewalked by. It's like playing solitaire,
slapping the red jack on the black queen;
king buried under the wrong pile.

I play on the bed; cards topple over when the dog
jumps on. She'll step right into my game
lick my face, wag her tail, till I deal again.

There is no game where my whole body
moves in one motion to its end.
There is one game where my whole body
moves in one motion to its end.

Woman on the Beach at Duxbury

Taking comfort in the spaniel beside her, she scans
the fence posts for the snowy owl, wonders if the
    dog
will scare it away. But an explosion of sunset
obscures her view, and she turns to the deep sea
    shadow
of the sea. Sniffing along aside her, floppy ears
    trailing
over snow covered sand, the dog's propelled
    forward.
How definitively it moves, backtracks,
then moves on again, not unlike memory,
some phantom scent pulling it along.

She's on the top step of the screened-in porch
with a blue striped ceramic bowl on her head.
Mother, ruddy-faced and sweaty, snips carefully,
"Stand still or your bangs will be crooked. "
Intent on finishing this task, her mother prods
the dull edge of scissors across the flesh of her
    forehead.
She jerks; scissors go askew.
A chunk of hair falls to the cement floor.
Her fault, her fault, the bangs too short,
the scold now repeating itself to low tide waves.

How silly, she chides herself oblivious to the
    evening chill.
Older now than that young mother, a mother
    four years dead,
she longs for the comfort of a chat, anything
    superficial —
the dog, the snowy owl just up the way.
White-feathered apparition stilted on an old
    fence post –
alert to it, she might distinguish it from the dunes.

Yearning in Four Parts

1.

What the Body Wants

Appetite, always appetite:
two forms rumpled into one another
sweat suffused into their frayed quilt.

or the odor of caramelized onions in a copper pan,
on the counter, a slab of salmon fillet —
its Northwest spawning, the long swim upstream
before being caught, not even imaginable
in this pink flesh.

What the Body Needs

To wade like the blue heron in a derelict field
slate shade of water and reed

to stop and elongate its neck,
before lifting off,

weightless mass
barely able to sustain itself
in the cross current of late winter.

3.

What the Heart Needs

In a childhood bedroom
thick-toothed linoleum clowns smiled up
from under the jacks. She can remember
the padded bounce of a small rubber ball,
her five year old fingers not deft enough to extricate
the star-shaped objects in twos, threes, fours...

What could the heart want
beyond the soft iambic pump:
ba bum, ba bum, ba bum.

4.

What the Soul Needs

Her mother died on the equinox
while she drove the old canyon road
toward the hospital, switchback curves
hard to maneuver in the pitch dark.
What struck her: how lush, the desert drafts
against her bare skinned arms — back home,
snow seven inches deep sodden into her garden.

How the thaw startles her:
as if buds erupted on dogwood
or yellow splurges of daffodil
shatter the sanctuary
of a life cocooned.

Acknowledgments

"Floundering," *Nimrod International Journal,* Tulsa, Oklahoma, Fall/Winter 1996

"Solitaire," finalist, 1996 Nimrod/Hardman Awards, *Nimrod International Journal,* Fall/Winter 1996.

"An Odd Elegy for my Mom" (Forgiveness), *Footwork: Paterson Literary Review* '92, Poetry Center, Passaic County Community College, Paterson, NJ, 1992

"Orchids," Honorable Mention, Awards Anthology, Poetry Center, Passaic County Community College, July 1991

"Prayer Basket," "Shoreline in the Late Afternoon," and "At the Veteran's Cemetery," *Footwork:* 1991

"The Blue Mug" (Courage), *Footwork,* Fall 1990

"The Christmas Photo," *Lips*, Fall 1989

"For My Unborn Daughter," *Southern Poetry Review*, Spring 1989

"Araivapa Canyon," *Footwork '88*

"Cafe Tres Bien," *Footwork '87*, Finalist poem, National Writers Union, Spring '86

"Older Woman," *Lactuca*, Spring '86

"Chasing Spirits," *Croton Review* Poetry Contest, 2nd prize, 1984

About the Author

PRISCILLA ORR is a recipient of fellowships from the Woodrow Wilson National Fellowship Foundation, Writers Workshop at Princeton University, and the New Jersey State Council on the Arts/Department of State. From 1984-96, Orr taught graduate poetry courses and women's studies as well as writing and literature courses at William Paterson College. A graduate of the University of Montana, Orr has an M.A. in English from Columbia University's Teachers College and an M.F.A. in poetry from Warren Wilson College in North Carolina. Her poetry has been published in *Southern Poetry Review, Bitterroot International Poetry Quarterly, Nimrod International Journal,* and *Croton Review*. Orr has been a resident at Yaddo writers colony in Saratoga Springs, New York. Raised in Mississippi and Montana, she resides with her spaniel in New Jersey and teaches at Bloomfield College. This is the first collection of her poetry.

Gen 0902121 70